Raiders of the
Dome Diamond

The Spirals Series

Plays

Jan Carew
Computer Killer

Chris Culshaw
Gaffs and Laughs
Radio Riff-Raff

Julia Donaldson
Books and Crooks

Nigel Gray
An Earwig in the Ear

Angela Griffiths
TV Hospital
Wally and Co

Paul Groves
Tell Me Where it Hurts

Julia Pattison
Kicking Up a Stink

Bill Ridgway
Monkey Business

John Townsend
A Bit of a Shambles
Chef's Night Off
Clogging the Works
Cowboys, Jelly and Custard
Gulp and Gasp
Hiccups and Slip-ups
Jumping the Gun
A Lot of Old Codswallop
Murder at Muckleby Manor

David Walke
The Good, the Bad and the Bungle
Package Holiday

Non-fiction

Jim Alderson
Crash in the Jungle

Chris Culshaw
Dive into Danger
Ground Zero

David Orme
Hackers

Jill Ridge
Lifelines

Bill Ridgway
Break Out!
Lost in Alaska
Over the Wall

Julie Taylor
Lucky Dip

John Townsend
Burke and Hare: The Body Snatchers
Kingdom of the Man-eaters
Raiders of the Dome Diamond

Keith West
Back to the Wild

Fiction

Jim Alderson
The Witch Princess

Penny Bates
Tiger of the Lake

Jan Carew
Footprints in the Sand
Voices in the Dark

Susan Duberley
The Ring

John Goodwin
Ghost Train

Angela Griffiths
Diary of a Wild Thing
Stories of Suspense

Anita Jackson
The Actor
The Austin Seven
Bennet Manor
Dreams
The Ear
A Game of Life and Death
No Rent to Pay

Paul Jennings
Eye of Evil
Maggot

Richard Kemble
Grandmother's Secret

Helen Lowerson
The Biz

Margaret Loxton
The Dark Shadow

Bill Ridgway
The Hawkstone
Mr Punch
Spots

John Townsend
Back on the Prowl
A Minute to Kill
Night Beast
Snow Beast
Sweet Dreams

NON-FICTION

Raiders of the Dome Diamond

John Townsend

Text © John Townsend 2003

The right of John Townsend to be identified as the author of this work has been asserted by him in accordance with the Copyright, Designs and Patents Act 1988.

All rights reserved. No part of this publication may be reproduced or transmitted in any form or by any means, electronic or mechanical, including photocopy, recording or any information storage and retrieval system, without permission in writing from the publisher or under licence from the Copyright Licensing Agency Limited, 90 Tottenham Court Road, London W1T 4LP.

Any person who commits any unauthorised act in relation to this publication may be liable to criminal prosecution and civil claims for damages.

Published in 2003 by:
Nelson Thornes Ltd
Delta Place
27 Bath Road
CHELTENHAM
GL53 7TH
United Kingdom

03 04 05 06 07 / 10 9 8 7 6 5 4 3 2 1

A catalogue record for this book is available from the British Library

ISBN 0 7487 7244 8

Cover illustration by Jim Eldridge
Page make-up by Tech-Set, Gateshead

Printed in Croatia by Zrinski

1

7 November 2000
London

A van moved slowly along West Ferry Road. It was towing a speedboat towards the River Thames. The sun began to shine through the thin morning mist. The van stopped beside the river. Two men got out and lowered the boat into the dark water. Without saying a word, the driver got back in the van and sped away.

Just after 8 am, the van pulled into a coal yard in south-east London. The driver parked it next to a shed.

It was just another Tuesday. People were on their way to work. No one took much notice as the van driver opened the shed doors. No one gave a thought as the boat on the river roared into life.

The boat sped down-river towards Greenwich. It cut through the waves and headed for the Millennium Dome.

A woman looked down from her office window. She saw the boat skim the water. She gave a shrug and went to her desk. The river was full of boats. This was just one more.

A roar came from the shed in the coal yard. A yellow digger chugged into the daylight. Its driver stared out at the road ahead. His eyes were bright. This was the day he'd been waiting for. He drove the digger into a quiet street and began to head for the Dome.

At the Blackwall Tunnel, the digger came to a stop. Three men climbed inside. The digger's cabin had been made bigger. Now it could hold all four of them. The men had also worked on the digger to make it go faster. Now they were roaring off towards the Millennium Dome.

A tall wire fence ringed the Dome. The digger swung around and crashed right through the fence. People looked up in shock. The fence lay flat under the machine's huge wheels. The digger picked up speed in a blast of black smoke. Nothing could stop it. With a crash, it rammed Gate 4 of the Dome.

On the river at Millennium Pier, the boat was waiting. The pilot had his hands on the controls. He was ready to make a fast getaway. The fastest of his life.

It would be worth it. Worth the risk. If things went well, he'd be a rich man before the day was out. They'd all be millionaires.

2

31 December 1999
London

'Five ... four ... three ... two ... one!' It was midnight. The crowds cheered. Fireworks flashed over the River Thames. Sparks sprayed the London sky. Big Ben struck 12 and the crowds roared. The old century was over. A new millennium had begun.

A big party was underway at the Millennium Dome. The Queen and Prime Minister were there. This was the place to celebrate the year 2000. Now it would be open to the public. Over the next year, crowds would mark the new age by seeing the Dome's big displays.

The Dome was huge. There was a lot to see. You could wander through the Body Zone or the Mind Zone. You could watch acrobats or dancers. Or you could go to the Money Zone and gasp at the Millennium Star. It was the diamond of all diamonds. It was as big as an egg. And it was worth a fortune.

The TV cameras were all there. The diamond was to go on show for the first time. Drums rolled. Cameras flashed. The crowds cheered.

The spotlights came on and the Millennium Star glinted in a rainbow of colours. The crowd gasped. The diamond was huge. It was stunning. No one had seen anything like it before.

Now the spotlights were dimmed as laser beams hit the sparkling gem. Shafts of dazzling light filled the Dome. The great jewel was a shower of silver sparks.

A girl from the latest James Bond film posed for the cameras. *The World is Not Enough* was filmed at the Millenium Dome. The film had a river chase in speedboats. There was smoke and gunshots. James Bond had to dive from an air balloon on to the roof of the Dome. It was all part of the plot. No one knew then how real the story would get.

A new story was soon to put the Dome on to TV screens again. And the star would be that famous diamond.

3

January 2000
The Old Kent Road, London

Four men sat smoking in a dim room above a pub. Beer cans stood on the table among the maps and photos. Each man looked into the eyes of those sitting round the table. Who could be trusted?

Two of the men had worked together before. But this was their first job of the New Year. Their plan was to rob a van full of cash. They'd hold up the van by the Dogs' Home in Battersea. After grabbing £10 million, they'd run for it. They'd make a fast getaway. Easy.

One of the men crushed a beer can and threw it into the corner. He pointed to a street map.

'No good. Too much traffic. We'd never get away in time. That street gets blocked. It can't be done.'

'Who said anything about streets?' A man with a shaved head slowly moved his finger to the map. It rested on the word THAMES. He smiled.

'The river is the best way. A boat will do the job in half the time. I know where to get a good one.'

He struck a match and lit a cigar. Smoke rose in a fog around the light bulb. The others squinted through the haze. This man was the boss. No one questioned him. He poured a glass of whisky and put it to his lips. He drank it in one gulp.

'And I'll tell you something else . . .' He looked at their faces in turn.

'This job's only the start. This is just a game to sort the men from the boys. The next job is the big one.'

4

11 February 2000
Nine Elms Road, Battersea, London

Just before 7 am, a man shut his front door and went out to his car. He was late for work and in a rush. When he got to the kerb, he swore. A lorry was parked in front of his car. There was no way he could get his car out. He was in no mood for this. He stormed over to the lorry to tell the driver what he thought.

The driver wasn't there. The man tried the cab door. It was open and the keys were inside. He grabbed the keys in a rage and walked off to catch a bus. He turned the corner of the street just as a van drove past. A van full of cash.

Suddenly a BMW car pulled up in front of it. The van driver slammed on his brakes. Three men with guns ran from the car to the van. They wore hard hats. In seconds, four more men ran from a side street. They had a big steel cutter. The van driver could only sit in horror . . . and wait.

Sparks flew as the men cut the van's power cables under its back axle. Now it couldn't be driven away. All that was left was to cut open the side and grab the cash. The steel cutter would do the job. It would be as easy as using a can opener. But it was taking too long. The noise was too loud. At any moment they'd be seen. They'd have to use the lorry.

One of the robbers ran up the street to where the lorry was parked. Hidden under its load was a secret weapon – a sharp metal spike which stuck out of the back. The spike was welded to the body of the lorry. If the robber reversed the lorry at full speed into the van, the spike would ram a hole in its side. All that lovely cash would be theirs for the taking!

The robber jumped into the lorry cab. He reached for the keys. They weren't there. He emptied his pockets. He looked under the cab. It was too late. People were watching. The gang began to panic. There was nothing they could do. They had to get away – fast.

With screams and shouts, the robbers let off fire bombs. Flames ripped through the BMW and their lorry. They turned and ran like mad to the river. A few minutes later they were racing across the River Thames in a speedboat.

They escaped in a spray of foam while a cloud of smoke rose above Nine Elms Road.

5

Late February 2000
New Scotland Yard

The police were puzzled. Why had the gang run off without the cash? They knew they'd set fire to the car and lorry to get rid of any clues. But why did they escape by speedboat? That really got the police thinking. This gang had style.

Jon Shatford led the police team. He was head of the Flying Squad ('The Sweeney') at New Scotland Yard. He knew the gang would be back. They'd planned the raid well. They'd used a speedboat to make a fast exit. He felt they were checking out this way of escape. Would their next raid be somewhere else on the river? Perhaps. But where? Next time, these men might use their guns. A gang of thugs on the loose in London was bad news. They had to be stopped.

Nine Elms Road had been like a war zone. Flames and smoke had filled the street. People were in shock. Anyone could have been hurt. But who was behind it all?

The police began a huge search. They had to look at hundreds of records. It was a massive task. One of the crime workers spent weeks going through computer files.

He looked at data from hundreds of crimes. He tried to match the clues of the Nine Elms Road raid with known robbers.

After months of work, he saw a link. It was just a chance. One name came up on his computer screen. He ran into Jon Shatford's office. 'Sir! I think I've got someone.'

The name was Ray Betson. He was a big-time crook who lived in Kent. Police thought he was behind many armed robberies around London. He'd also been in prison in the past. The printout made interesting reading.

> Ray Betson, born 1961. Known as 'The General'. Owns flats in Canary Wharf, London. Also owns flats in Spain. House in Kent is worth £500,000. Spent £25,000 flying to New York on Concorde for a Millennium party. No job. A millionaire. All his money is from robbery, drug smuggling and other crimes. **DANGEROUS**.

Another detail now went on the file.

> Ray Betson. Main suspect in failed robbery on 11 February 2000 in Nine Elms Road. May strike again. Could be soon. **ALERT.**

6

Summer 2000
The Old Kent Road, London

Ray Betson lit a cigarette and threw the match on to the table. It fell between a map and a small book. The title could just be seen in the dimly lit room: *A Day Out at the Dome*.

A smoky haze hung above the four men's heads. The biggest man held a pint of beer in one hand and the book in the other. He grunted as he turned the pages. There were photos on every page.

He stopped turning the pages and smiled. He'd found what he was looking for. The title on the page was 'The Millennium Star Diamond'.

Ray drew on his cigarette. 'So, what do you reckon, Will?'

Will took a swig of beer. 'Nice. Very nice. I wouldn't mind getting my hands on this one.'

Aldo sat in the corner looking at the map. He was restless. He thumped the table, making the glasses jump. Whisky splashed over the map. 'Mad! You're all crazy. You'll never do it. Mad!'

The fourth man was much older. He'd been making notes on a pad. He had drawings of tractors and diggers. After stubbing out a cigarette in the ashtray, he looked at Betson. 'It's risky, Ray. It's a hell of a risk. But we can do it. And if we do . . .'

Ray smiled. 'If we do, Bob, we'll be very rich men. We'll never have to do another job. Ever. It'll be the biggest raid of all time. All we need are a couple of drivers and we'll get away with the queen of diamonds!'

'But what if we don't?' Aldo said as he poured himself a whisky. 'What if we don't get away? What if we fail?'

Ray's dark eyes stared through the smoke. There was danger in his soft voice. 'That's not a word I think about, Aldo. I don't fail.'

'But what about last time?' The words came out before Aldo could stop them.

Ray hit the table. 'And whose fault was that? We won't make the same mistake twice. This time it's just us.'

Bob put down his glass. 'The thing is, Ray . . . lifting this little gem is one thing. Getting rid of it is another.'

'Don't you worry about that, Bob. I've already seen to it. I've got a buyer.' Ray tapped his nose. 'Oh yes, I've got contacts. Two hundred million in cash. Think of it.'

Aldo went to the window and looked outside. He was on edge. He didn't know who might be out there.

'Relax, Aldo,' Ray said. 'Trust me. We can pull this off.'

'But what about the alarms? The Dome must be wired up like the Bank of England.'

'Maybe there's a bit of security. We can deal with that. It'll be like taking candy from a baby. Show him, Will.'

Will picked up a bag from under the table. He took out a nail gun. 'This will go through thick glass like butter. A couple of shots and a blow with a sledge hammer and the case will fall apart. It'll only take seconds. Simple.'

Aldo looked Will in the eyes. 'If it's that easy, why hasn't someone tried to grab the diamond before?' He took one more look out of the window. 'I mean, how can you be so sure?'

Ray butted in. 'We'll show you. You'll see how easy it is. I've got us all tickets to the Dome. We'll pay a visit. Have a day out. I'll video the lot and we'll study it. You'll see I'm right. Honest.'

Aldo smiled and shook his head. 'You . . . honest? Now you must be joking!' He looked from one man to the other. From Ray Betson to Will Cockram to Bob Adams. His eyes rested on the photo of the Millennium Star. 'OK,' he said. 'Count me in.'

7

September 2000
Greenwich, London

The Millennium Dome was already busy. Schoolchildren and tourists lined up to get inside. It was buzzing with action. Security guards mixed with the crowds. There were cameras in every zone, on the lookout for pickpockets and thieves.

Ray Betson aimed his camcorder at the Money Zone. He looked like any other tourist. He filmed inside the strongroom where the diamond was on show. Will Cockram was already admiring the diamond. At least, that's what he seemed to be doing. In fact, he was looking closely at the thick glass case. He was working out the best way to smash a hole in the side.

Aldo and Bob weren't far behind. They were noting the layout of the Dome. While Bob worked out how far the Money Zone was from all the exits, Aldo drew a quick map. They had to know the fastest way to get into the diamond room and out to the river. Every second would count.

Aldo stopped drawing his plan. He felt a security camera pointing at him. He tried to relax, to look like a normal tourist. Like his mate, Bob. Bob was walking around with an ice cream in one hand and a guide book in the other. It seemed as if they didn't have a care in the world. The camera fixed on Aldo for a few seconds and moved on.

Up in the control room, the wall of screens showed all parts of the Dome. Security staff watched the pictures flash in front of them. Some pushed buttons to control the cameras. The police had told them to keep a close lookout. There was a chance Ray Betson and his gang were planning a raid somewhere near the river. Betson's photo had been pinned up near the screens.

One of the security staff was watching the screen showing the Millennium Star. 'That big guy likes the look of the diamond,' he said. 'He's been looking at it quite a while. He knows a gem when he sees one. A bit like that guy over there with his camcorder. Hang on a minute . . . it's him. It's Ray Betson!'

The guard made the camera zoom in on Ray's face. The control room went mad. The name 'Betson' buzzed through the Dome in seconds. A call was made to New Scotland Yard. The police were told straight away. The Dome was on red alert.

*Autumn 2000
New Scotland Yard*

Jon Shatford's hunch was right. He'd warned his police team to keep watch along the River Thames. Now they knew. Ray Betson and his gang were after the Dome diamond. He'd been filmed. He was planning a raid. It was time to act.

The Flying Squad got to work. Operation 'Magician' was soon under way. First they took a close look at the video tapes showing Ray Betson and Will Cockram at the Dome. They spotted another man acting in an odd way. He was filming the outside of the Dome and the Millennium Pier.

Jon Shatford was in no doubt. These men were going to rob the Dome of its famous diamond. It seemed too mad to be true. Just how would they do it? And when?

The police had to be ready. They'd have to catch the gang red-handed. But how? The public would be at risk. So would the staff at the Dome. This gang was violent. Once Ray and his mates had a plan, nothing would stop them.

Hundreds of police rushed to the Dome. They were dressed as tourists or cleaners. They couldn't risk scaring off the gang. Many of the police were armed. They hid guns in litter bins or under food stands. They set up cameras in the Dome, in the streets and along the river. Every corner was watched.

The Dome bosses were told to do their jobs as normal. But they'd have to make one change. The Millennium Star and the other diamonds had to go – without anyone knowing. Fake diamonds were put in the case, just to be on the safe side.

Day after day the police watched and waited. Nothing. Were they wrong after all? Jon Shatford was sure a speedboat would come into it somewhere. He looked at a chart showing the tides on this part of the river. It would have to be a high tide to let the boat get in close. The next high tide was on 6 November. He was sure the attack would be then. 6 November 2000. That was the day to be ready . . . and waiting.

The police filmed a digger in a nearby coal yard. It drove around the yard from time to time. It seemed as if it was on a trial run. A speedboat sometimes rushed up to the Millennium Pier before shooting up river again. They filmed the boat, too.

On the morning of 6 November the digger left the yard. It headed towards the Dome. All police officers rushed to their places. A signal was given. Operation Magician was

'GO'. The Flying Squad sped to the scene and waited. Jon Shatford had no idea how the gang would strike. The mood was electric.

Nothing happened. The digger turned and went back to its shed. The raid was off. All went quiet. Perhaps the gang had got wind of the police. Had they picked up a radio signal? Did they have a spy inside the Dome? What was going on?

Life at the Millennium Dome carried on as normal. The fake gems glinted in their case. The police kept on red alert. Jon Shatford waited. Night fell. The gates were locked. Would the raid be at midnight? The Flying Squad couldn't rest.

That night, Ray Betson and Will Cockram sat in a pub. Each held a glass. Ray raised his with a grin. 'An early night is called for, Will. But first let me give a little toast, my friend.'

He clinked his glass against Will's. 'Tomorrow and the Star,' he said.

His mate gulped the whisky in one swig. He slammed the glass down on the table and wiped his mouth with the back of his hand. He grinned. 'Tomorrow and the Star!'

9

7 November 2000
The Millennium Dome

Just after 9.30 am the digger crashed through Gate 4 and headed right for the Dome. The four men in the cab wore helmets. They held on, waiting for the crunch. A fifth man was not far away. His name was Kevin Meredith. He was waiting in the speedboat to rush them away. On the other side of the river a sixth man sat in a van. He was ready to drive them and the diamonds to a hideout.

The raid was about to begin. In the Dome, undercover police were on red alert. A team of armed police hid outside the Money Zone.

The digger smashed through the side of the Dome in a shower of glass and metal. Groups of children were moved out of the way. Other visitors were told to keep well away from the diamonds. If people had been standing nearby, they'd have been flattened.

Nothing could stop the machine as it charged through the wall at 20 miles per hour. It screamed to a stop and the four men jumped out. They wore gas masks and bright workmen's jackets. Ray Betson jumped from the cab, shouting, 'Attack! Attack! Attack!'

Will Cockram and Bob Adams ran to the diamond case. Will got there first. He wore a thick bullet-proof jacket and carried a heavy nail gun. Bob was close behind. He had two sledge hammers, some bottles of ammonia and a bolt cutter. Their job was to grab the jewels while Ray and Aldo kept people away from the digger. They'd need it to speed off again. They'd smash through another wall and get away on the speedboat.

The glass case should have been bullet proof. It should have taken half an hour for anyone to get inside. Will and Bob took just 30 seconds. The blast of the nail gun from close-up ripped through the glass. Will fired three times. The sledge hammers did the rest. It took just two blows to make a hole big enough to grab the Millennium Star. Or what they thought was the Millennium Star.

As Will and Bob worked on the glass case, Aldo threw smoke bombs. People ran for cover. Through the fog came the noise of shouting and the roar of the digger. It was just as the gang had planned. If anyone tried to stop them, they'd use the ammonia. One spray in the eyes would be enough.

But there was no need. Everything was going well. Very well. There'd been no hold-ups. In fact, they were faster than planned. What could go wrong? It was a push-over.

10

7 November 2000
The Money Zone

Jon Shatford gave the order. Armed police sprang from nowhere. Other police, dressed as cleaners, grabbed guns from bin liners and ran into the strongroom. One word rang out: 'FREEZE!'

Will and Bob fell to the floor. It was over before they could grab their prize. Now all they could do was lie face-down on the floor, with their arms handcuffed behind their backs.

Ray and Aldo had been keeping watch by the digger. Suddenly men with guns ran through the smoke. In seconds Ray and Aldo were in handcuffs too. The game was up.

Ray Betson had planned the raid for months. He'd spent £300,000 to set it up. Now he just lay there. It had all gone wrong. He shut his eyes and said nothing. He was wondering who'd shopped him. Anger rose in his face.

Outside the Dome more police rushed to the Millennium Pier. They grabbed the man in the speedboat. Others rushed to get the van driver across the river. He, too, was under arrest. Within minutes, the whole of Operation Magician was over. Six men had been caught red-handed. Not a gun had been fired. The only man hurt was Will Cockram. He had a black eye.

The smoke from Aldo's bombs drifted away. People crept out from their hiding places. They stared as the four men inside the Money Zone were led to the waiting police cars. The Dome fell still as the police left the scene. Everyone gave a sigh of relief. The Dome had been on red alert 24 times in two months while police waited for the robbers to strike. Now it was all over.

Jon Shatford had taken a big risk. The ambush could have gone wrong, but it had paid off. Ray Betson took an even bigger risk. He'd failed.

It could have been very different. The look on Betson's face said it all. He later said he was proud of his record. He'd been an armed robber for 20 years and had never been caught. This time his luck had run out.

As he was led away, Bob Adams looked back at the Money Zone. He shook his head. 'I was just inches away from payday. It would've been a blinding Christmas!'

11

November 2001
The Old Bailey, London

It took a year for the case to reach court. Security was tight. Armed police stood on guard each day outside Number 2 Court at the Old Bailey. The men on trial were violent. Their friends might try to help them.

Five men went on trial: Raymond Betson (40 years old), William Cockram (49), Robert Adams (57), Aldo Ciarrocchi (32) and Kevin Meredith (34). The sixth member of the gang died before the trial. He was the driver of the getaway van.

The trial lasted over three months. Christmas came and went. The jury went to the Dome to look at the scene of the raid. It took a long time to hear the full story.

There was no doubt the men were guilty of trying to steal the Millennium Star. They were also guilty of trying to steal the 11 rare blue diamonds in the next case. If they'd got away with the lot, they'd have been the biggest robbers of all time. The diamonds were worth over £200 million.

There were videos of the gang being caught red-handed. The whole raid and the events leading up to it were on film. How could any of the men hope to be let off?

The big question was, were they guilty of theft or robbery? Theft is stealing. Robbery is using force to steal. 'Force' can mean using guns or putting people in danger. Plotting to rob is far more serious than plotting to steal. There was a long debate. Did these men set out to harm anyone?

To Jon Shatford's surprise, none of the men had guns. They'd had used them in the past. For some reason they left them in the van. Even so, people could have been hurt. A charging ten-tonne digger, a nail gun, sledge hammers, smoke bombs and ammonia bottles aren't very friendly! He'd no doubt these were violent men. If anyone had got in their way, the gang would have lashed out. A nail gun could kill someone in seconds.

At last, the judge began to sum up. The story was out in the open. It was now up to the jury to make up its mind.

12

February 2002
The Old Bailey, London

The jury of seven women and five men took seven days to reach a verdict. Yes, it was attempted robbery. Not theft. Four men were guilty of plotting to rob. Kevin Meredith, the boat driver, was guilty of plotting to steal. He hadn't been a danger to others. He told the court he'd been made to join the gang against his will.

On 18 February the judge passed sentence. He looked at the five men in front of him. His face was stern. 'You are evil criminals. You played for very high stakes. The police were waiting. The public has a lot to thank them for. It's only by luck that no one was hurt. This robbery was for a huge sum. If it had succeeded, it would have been the biggest robbery in the history of the world.'

The room was tense. Everyone waited for the judge to tell each man his sentence. 'Raymond Betson and William Cockram, you will both go to jail for 18 years. Robert Adams and Aldo Ciarrocchi, you will both go to jail for 15 years. Kevin Meredith, you are guilty of plotting to steal. You will be sent to jail for 5 years.'

There were mixed feelings in court. Many people were pleased. Some were shocked. Kevin Meredith's wife and mother sobbed. Ray Betson and Aldo Ciarrocchi had faces like stone. Will Cockram and Bob Adams smiled as they were led away to the cells.

That night the TV news told the whole story for the first time. The Dome Raid was hot news around the world. Next day the papers printed all the details. Some said it was a daring raid that nearly paid off. One of the most daring of all time.

Others said the idea was mad. The robbers were fools. They'd taken too many risks. They had more greed than sense. It was more like a comedy than a James Bond film. The real heroes were Jon Shatford and the Flying Squad.

Together, the five robbers were going to prison for 71 years between them. Seventy-one years is a long time to think about the Millennium Star.

It's a long time to remember how a perfect diamond was just out of reach. Even if it did turn out to be a worthless fake!

13

There's something about the way a diamond seems to wink and flash. Crooks have always wanted to steal them.

There's a magic about all diamonds. They dazzle. They sparkle. They shine for ever. That's why they were chosen to mark the New Millennium.

A diamond will last for all time. And now the Dome Raiders have all the time in the world. Time to think. Time to remember the day they tried to steal the Millennium Star.

Time to regret their big mistake.

This book made use of newspaper articles of the period, including Nick Parker and Mike Sullivan in the *Sun* (8 November 2000), and the *Sun*, *The Times* and the *Telegraph* (19 February 2002). Other information can be found on Internet websites such as:

- Ananova
  (www.ananova.com/news/story/sm_108842.html)

- BBC News
  (news.bbc.co.uk/hi/english/static/in_depth/uk/2000/diamond_raid/default.stm)

- Guardian Unlimited
  (www.guardian.co.uk/dome/article/0,2763,393971,00.html)
  (www.guardian.co.uk/dome/article/0,2763,394044,00.html).